W9-DBN-712

For Oliver and August
And my grandchildren-to-come,
Their parents and mine,
And you.

You Do It Like This ...
I Did It Like That

REFLECTIONS OF "GRAND" YEARS

Written by P. Taylor Copeland
Illustrated by Erin Ambrose

You Do It Like This . . . I Did It Like That

© 2004 by Grammy Time™ Books
P.O. Box 639
San Luis Obispo, California 93406-0639
Message/Fax: (805) 541-3515
www.grammytimebooks.com

Designed by
[KRAFTWERK]DESIGN

Printed in China

First Edition September 2004
ISBN 0-9712675-3-7

You Do It Like This ...
I Did It Like That

Grandparent-To-Be

You're having a baby,
I'm a grandparent-to-be,
Memories flood back
Of just you and me.

Wasn't it yesterday
You sat on my lap?
Soon I will watch
Your child's life unwrap.

I'm bursting with pride,
I tell any and all —
"My grandchild is due,"
And I make a new call.

I reflect on times shared
And times ahead, too;
Grateful you'll know
How much I love you.

It's a joyous occasion:
A new love to behold,
But how can it be?
Am I really that old?

Expecting a Baby

Cravings, fatigue,
Mommy's belly is showing;
With each flutter, each kick,
The baby is growing.

A new little being
Is warming within,
Sharing a body
Until first breaths begin.

You worry about weight —
Too little, too much;
About labor, delivery
And the life you'll both touch.

You think about names,
Some girl and some boy;
You ready the nursery
For wonder and joy.

This new little heart
Beats just one touch away
While you fall in love
More and more everyday.

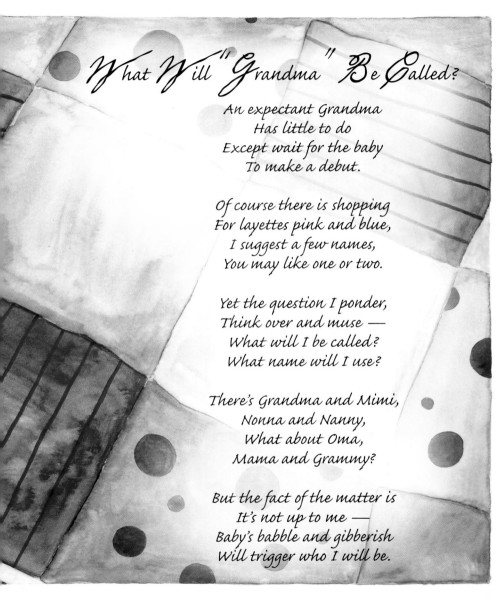

What Will "Grandma" Be Called?

An expectant Grandma
Has little to do
Except wait for the baby
To make a debut.

Of course there is shopping
For layettes pink and blue,
I suggest a few names,
You may like one or two.

Yet the question I ponder,
Think over and muse —
What will I be called?
What name will I use?

There's Grandma and Mimi,
Nonna and Nanny,
What about Oma,
Mama and Grammy?

But the fact of the matter is
It's not up to me —
Baby's babble and gibberish
Will trigger who I will be.

7

Celebrating Hormones

When you were a teen
With hormones askew,
Emotions ran rampant,
Mood swings were all new.

Each natural transition
A part of life's change,
But this is a dance
That can feel a bit strange.

You may feel it again
As a mommy-to-be,
First trimester explosions
Bring tears and then glee.

At least with this change
You have a baby to show —
My rite of passage
Leaves hot flashes and glow.

But, "This too shall pass,"
I think with a snicker,
We're each growing older —
I'll just get there quicker.

9

Labor and Birth

The baby is coming,
It's on the way.
Ready or not
Today is the day.

You time the contractions,
They're two minutes apart;
The suitcase is packed,
It's time to depart.

Breathe in, breathe deep,
You labor a shout,
"This really sucks!"
Pant, pant, and blow out.

And then with some pushing
Your baby arrives.
A new breath of love
Now enters our lives.

A beautiful miracle,
A blessed event,
And the pain that was there —
Is a child heaven sent.

Grandparent's First Glimpse

I anxiously wait
As the hours tick by;
At long last it happens:
I hear baby's first cry.

My grandchild is here,
A joy to my world,
Sweetness and love
Newly born and unfurled.

My eyes fill with tears
As we meet the first time,
You surrender this newborn
From your arms to mine.

I'm holding the future
Wrapped all nice and tight,
Mixed with Mommy's perfection
And Daddy's delight.

This child of my child,
A beacon of light —
I am over the moon,
It's a love at first sight.

13

New Baby Jitters

Baby is home!
You're all on your own.
Mommy and Daddy
Undertake the unknown.

Not quite as certain
As you thought you would be,
New baby jitters
Bring phone calls to me.

Baby's first bath
Gives Daddy concern,
And baby's first outing
Ends in early return.

Mommy talks mostly
Of baby's pooping and eating.
While sleep deprivation
Is somewhat defeating.

But just one little snuggle
With this child you adore
And you don't mind at all
Waking at twelve, two, and four.

15

Grandma Sitting

Mommy and Daddy
Are out on a date,
Just baby and me —
Isn't it great?

Don't get me wrong,
I enjoy my kids too,
But my time with this baby
Is long overdue.

I've saved extra snuggles,
They're ready to use,
And brought peek-a-boo games
To entertain and amuse.

My "rock-a-bye baby"
Should soothe every cry,
But if that doesn't work
I've got more tricks to try.

I relish our moments,
Both awake and asleep,
Because I've been here before
And know babies don't keep.

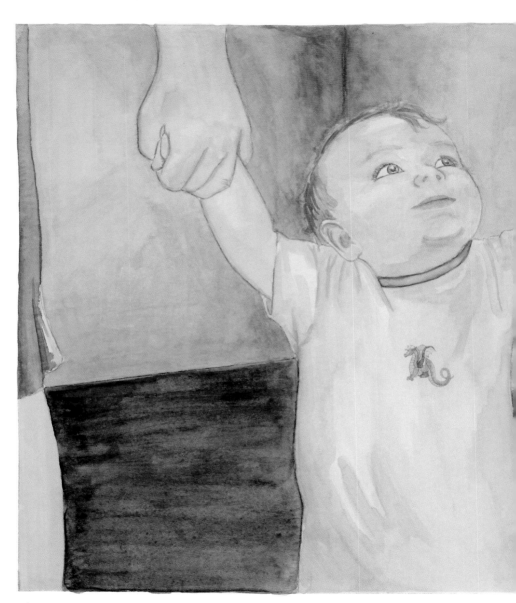

17

Mommy and Daddy

A mommy gives kisses
For a bump on the knee;
A daddy protects
With love's guarantee.

A mommy is warmth
With affection and care;
A daddy is strength
With a determined, kind air.

A mommy is gentle
Using patience to guide;
A daddy is playful
With expectation and pride.

A mommy has eyes
In the back of her head;
A daddy has radar
And awareness widespread.

United as parents
For the child they esteem,
Mommy and Daddy,
Each part of a team.

Photographs

Brag Book

First Steps

Coos and new giggles,
A small clutching fist,
Baby rolls over
Without an assist.

From crawling all over
To first steps alone,
I shamelessly brag
Making each triumph well known.

This child is a genius,
There's no doubt in my mind,
A new little star
With perfection combined.

Reaching each milestone
A matter of pride,
Not for the child,
But for me on the side.

I watch from afar,
I watch with delight —
But I wish I were nearer
To say "nighty-night."

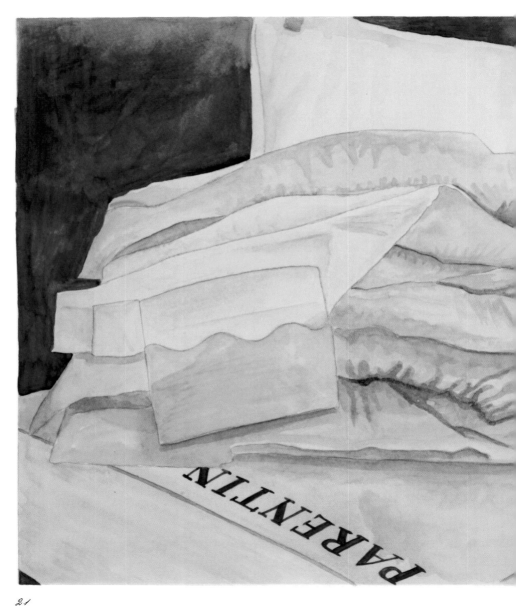

PARENTIN

You Do It Like This...
I Did It Like That

When you were a baby,
Not that long ago,
We weren't quite as wise,
We just didn't know.

You slept on your tummy,
For goodness sake,
And with an unbelted car seat
My arm was your brake.

There's been lots of change
From then until now,
The evolution of parenting
Expands our know-how.

New-fangled gadgets
Sit where old-fashioned sat —
You do it like this . . .
I did it like that.

There's more than one way
To guide and to do,
But keep it consistent,
With lots of love, too.

Second Child

Pitter-patter, pitter-patter,
Little feet on the floor,
The firstborn child you love so much —
Soon, just one, no more.

A baby brother or baby sister
Is growing and on the way.
The stork is coming yet again
With a newborn child to stay.

The pregnant woes you felt before
No longer worry you now,
Not that you don't care as much,
There's just not time somehow.

Celebrating parenthood
For a second time
Attaches a brand new concern
Along with the sublime.

You can't imagine love enough —
Is there room for two?
Yes, love will always multiply
With each new child's debut.

Before Kids, After Kids

Before you had kids
You could sleep until noon,
Take a long shower,
Take a trip to Cancun.

You talked about work
And intellectual stuff;
A cat on your lap
Seemed, oddly, enough.

Things are now different,
Life's filled to the brim —
It's diapers and laundry
Instead of the gym.

Cartoons now replace
Your favorite newscast:
You step over toys
And eat very fast.

Your world's reinvented,
It's not what you knew,
But life without kids?
What on Earth would you do?

Playdates with Grandma

We go for long walks,
All the chores left undone,
My grandchild and I,
Having one-on-one fun.

We build castles of sand,
I answer, "What's that?"
We collect pinecones and seashells,
And jump in puddles that splat.

Everyday things
Now seen through fresh eyes,
It's an all-new perspective
And an unparalleled prize.

We dance and we sing,
Plant a vegetable patch,
Eat ice cream for dinner,
And make cookies from scratch.

There's no rushing to do,
It's a playdate with care,
But when this little one goes home —
I fall in the chair.

Grandpa's World

A grandpa is gentle,
A grandpa is kind,
A grandpa is strong
With a tolerant mind.

His knee is a horsey,
His shoulders, a roost,
His hug is a safe haven
Should this child need a boost.

He plays lots of games,
Better than most,
And will rumble and tumble
And tell tales grandiose.

He offers the world
To a discovering eye,
And can be a best pal,
Giving answers to "Why?"

It's a kid-friendly spot
With space just "to do,"
It's decades of love,
It's memories for two.

Parenting Versus Grandparenting

Some say I'm spoiling,
I say I'm not,
It's my time to indulge
And share the time that I've got.

I play every game,
Say more yeses than nos,
Enchant and engage,
And never once presuppose.

It's up to you to give guidance,
To watch over and lead,
But I'll be a backup
If this child has a need.

My role as a grandparent
Is love with some slack,
To respect you as a parent,
And, yes, I'll stand back.

For as much as I love
This grandchild of mine,
I know your love is more,
But I'm next in line.

Subject: Hello!

Hello Grandma and Grandpa –

Thank you for the card you sent!

Staying in Touch

My time with this child,
The best of the best;
Away or nearby,
My life's treasure chest.

Grandparent and child:
Involvement defined.
Not always in sight,
But always in mind.

E-mails and faxes,
Cards sent with great care;
I look forward to visits,
Some here and some there.

I receive funny photos,
We exchange daily news,
We talk on the phone
About friends and our views.

Staying in touch
Requires a "want" and a "do" —
It's a love with no obstacles,
It's wisdom and new.

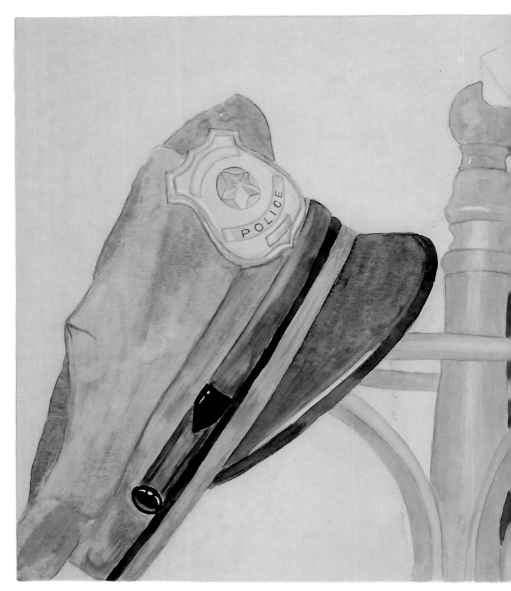

What is a Parent?

You're a caregiver, a nurse,
A teacher, and cook.
You're a chauffeur, and banker,
And a "Where-is-it" book.

You guide and you nurture
With listening ears;
You coach and you teach
And reconcile fears.

A first day of school
Brings tears to your eyes
And a last day commencement
Brings bittersweet sighs.

You're the giver of roots
On which to rely,
And the donor of wings
To reach for the sky.

You're a pillar of strength
Even when sad,
You're a number one fan —
You're a "Mom" or a "Dad."

Teen Years

Independence and struggles,
Self-image awry,
Rebellion and attitude,
And curfews — OH MY!

Your child is a teenager
Fitting life on for size —
Just trying to grow up
And to find what underlies.

Oh, how I remember
When you were this age.
Paybacks are tough,
It's a frustrating stage.

By adding "grand" to "parent"
I take on a new side,
I'm a defender and friend
With no judging: just pride.

I have kid-tested ears
And a soft place to fall —
Now, if only this child
Had time to visit or call.

BY MOM & DAD
TURN THAT DOWN!!

39

Linking the Generations

When I was a kid,
Some time ago,
We didn't have things
That are now status quo.

We didn't have cell phones,
VCRs, or PCs,
But doors were not locked
And we didn't need keys.

Elvis was nifty,
The Beatles were groovy,
Now it's CDs for music
And a DVD movie.

The past is our history,
The now is today,
The future our hope
As we each find our way.

By sharing our memories
And family's love bond,
We link generations
For this child and beyond.

Empty Nest

You stand in the driveway
Waving good-bye,
In the wake of a child
Now ready to fly.

The life that you made
Is now all but grown,
Plucking his dreams,
Going out on her own.

Beginnings and ends
Part of life's plan —
Girl becomes woman,
Boy becomes man.

With a pocket of memories
Your child leaves the nest.
Letting go isn't easy:
It takes time to digest.

But, I'll tell you a secret,
Though I know you are sad:
Unsung and new dreams
Are still yours to be had.

43

Someday When I am Gone

Someday when I am gone
It's important that you know
The love that's left in your heart
Is meant to grow and grow.

I'll leave you with our memories,
And the happy times we've had;
I hope that you will laugh and smile
And never feel too sad.

The love of generations,
Passed down from me to you,
Will encircle each new member
With a love that's tried and true.

A child is said to be a gift,
You brought me so much more;
And then you had a child
That I treasure and adore.

Each and every moment
You're in my heart to stay,
And because of that, when I am gone
I'll not be far away.

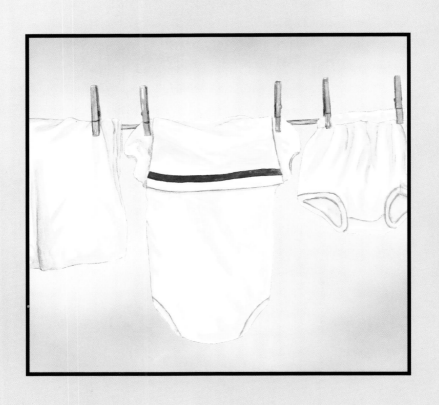

More from...

🖐 Grammy Time™ Books

For kids you love ~

Just You And Me
Let's Make-Believe

And grown-ups who care ~

I Liked You At Ten... I'll Like You Again
(Reflections of "Mommy" Years)

Visit www.grammytimebooks.com for more information.